ROME

ARCHAEOLOGICAL
GUIDE TO THE
ETERNAL CITY

WHITE STAR
PUBLISHERS

CHRONOLOGICAL TABLE

- *FOUNDATION*
753 BC   Traditional date for the founding of Rome
- *THE MONARCHY*
753 BC   Romulus
715   Numa Pompilius
673   Tullus Hostilius
642   Ancus Marcius
616   Tarquinius Priscus
578   Servius Tullius
535   Tarquinius Superbus
- *THE REPUBLIC*
509 BC   Foundation of the Republic
451   Laws of the Twelve Tables
421   The plebeians gain equal rights
396   Defeat of Veius
272   Fall of Tarantum (Taranto)
270   Beginning of expansion into the Mediterranean
202   End of the Second Punic War
146   Sack of Corinth. Destruction of Carthage
90/88   Social war
88/82   Civil war between Marius and Silla
49/45   Civil war between Pompey and Caesar
48 BC   Octavian
48/44   Dictatorship of Caesar
44/31   Civil war
- *THE EMPIRE*

31 BC	Caesar Octavian Augustus		249 AD	Decius
14 AD	Tiberius		251	Trebonianus Gallus
37	Caligula		253-60	Valerian
41	Claudius		253-67	Gallienus
54	Nero		268	Claudius Gothicus
68-9	Galba, Otho, Vitellius		270	Aurelianus
69	Vespasian		276	Probus
79	Titus		284	Diocletian - Maximinian
81	Domitian		305	Maximinian - Constantius
96	Nerva		306	Maxentius - Severus
98	Trajan		309/10	Galerius
117	Hadrian		312	Constantine
138	Antoninus Pius		337	Constantine II - Constans I - Constantius II
161	Marcus Aurelius		364	Valentinian I
180	Commodus		375	Gratianus
193	Septimius Severus		383	Valentinian II
211	Caracalla		395	Honorius
218	Elagabalus		423	Valentinian III
222	Alexander Severus		475	Romulus Augustolus
235	Maximinian		476	Odoacer
238	Gordian I, II, III		493	Theodoric
244	Philip the Arab			

THE MATERIALS

The Romans distinguished themselves from other ancient peoples by their construction skills, and left a legacy that to some extent survives to this day. The *De Architectura* by Vitruvius, a writer who lived during the era of Caesar and Augustus, provides a precious, exhaustive source of information on the architecture, engineering and general culture of ancient Rome.

The development of construction techniques in any civilization is closely related to the quality and quantity of material available in the area. Thus, during an older period when trade is not yet fully developed, it is natural for construction to be intimately connected to this factor, which of course also controls development. It is also true that the choice of construction materials is highly dependent on the type of building, its size and location, economic resources, and, last but not least, current tastes. Vitruvius indicates the qualities that had to be sought and pursued by architects in the form of three golden rules: *firmitas*, or solidity of the structures; *utilitas*, or functionality, which was based on how space was organized; and *venustas*, an elegant aesthetic appearance.

Because of the geo-morphological characteristics common throughout Lazio, the materials used beginning in the 7th century BC are quite similar. Using materials naturally available, rather simple structures were built, such as huts of reeds and clay with straw roofs. Later, rock such as tufa was used that was available and easy to quarry from the hills of the city.

Quarrymen worked in the quarries and

resistant blocks. With the end of the second century BC, travertine began to be used. This was considerably superior to other rocks due to its solidity and durability. Augustus then began experimenting with marble. He increased the quarries in Luni, in Etruria, which produced an excellent white marble that was shipped to Rome by sea as far as Ostia, and then sent up the Tiber.

used a simple tool to cut the rock horizontally and vertically to the required size, thus obtaining blocks that were sometimes finished on site. Some of the various rocks that Vitruvius mentions, such as tufa, had to be quarried in the summer and were then exposed to the air for two years before being used, to eliminate humidity and lead to the use of the most

Imported marble was used for the decorative parts of monuments such as columns, friezes, trabeations, floors and sculptures. It is said that, before dying, the emperor told his friends that he had inherited a city of bricks and had left one of marble.

Of course, many parts of buildings were still made of wood, including

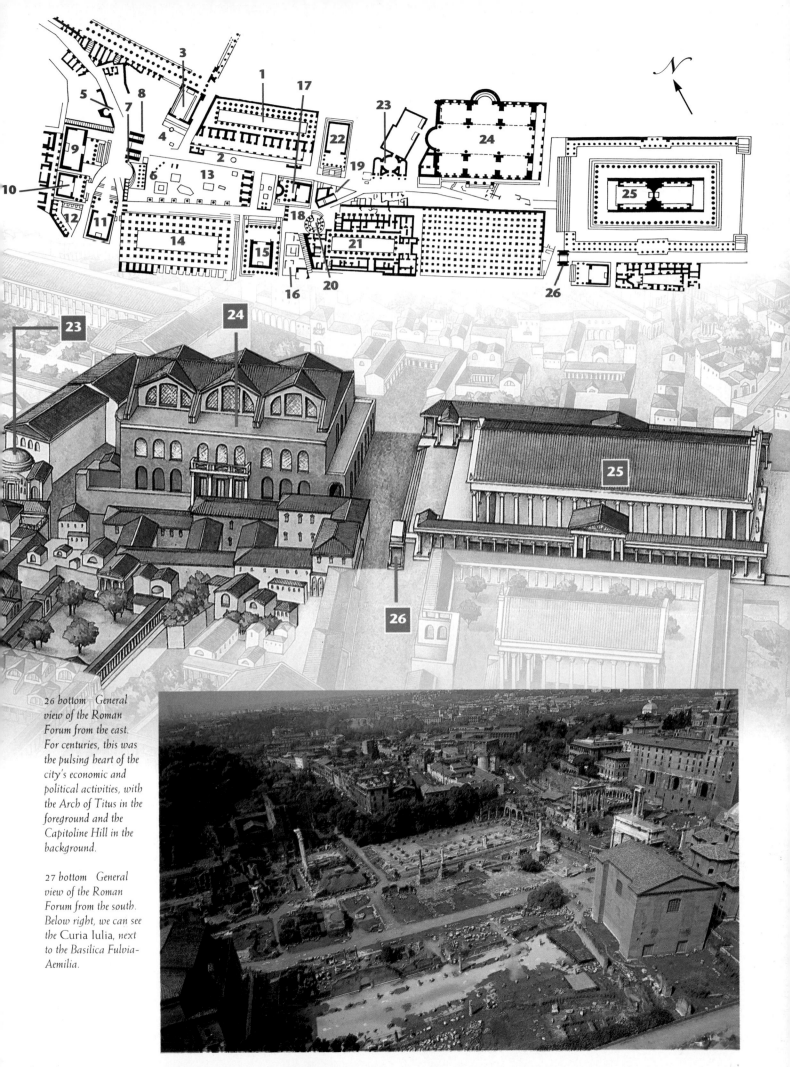

26 bottom   General view of the Roman Forum from the east. For centuries, this was the pulsing heart of the city's economic and political activities, with the Arch of Titus in the foreground and the Capitoline Hill in the background.

27 bottom   General view of the Roman Forum from the south. Below right, we can see the Curia Iulia, next to the Basilica Fulvia-Aemilia.

built, the so-called *Lapis Niger*, which tradition attributes to Numa Pompilius.

After the kings were driven from Rome (509 BC), new buildings were added in connection with the birth of new Republican institutions: the *Temple of Castor and Pollux*; the *Temple of Saturn*, with an avant-corps in which the Treasury was located; the speakers' platform, which became known as the Rostra after 338 BC, due to the prows (*rostra*) of the ships of Actium hanging here. Beginning in the 4th century BC, open space began to be occupied by so many columns and honorary statues that most of them had to be removed in the second century. The *Macellum* was built in the third century BC. It was a retail market located north of the Forum, and

forums, the supremacy and importance of the Forum Romanum gradually diminished. The last construction of any importance dates back to the 4th century AD, when Maxentius again chose Rome as his capital and built the great *Basilica*, the seat of the city prefect, and the so-called *Temple of Romulus*. During the High Middle Ages, many buildings were transformed into churches and fortresses, and the land became pasture for livestock. In the late 18th century, the excavations that led to the current layout began.

INFORMATION FOR VISITORS. You can begin your visit after getting an overall view of the *Forum Romanum* from the *Tabularium* arcades or the street that runs

was later replaced by the Temple of Peace. The great basilicas were then erected in the second century, introducing a new type of building that was destined to become a characteristic feature in Rome's urban landscape. A fifth building, the *Tabularium*, completed the scene for the Republican-era Forum toward the Capitoline Hill. Caesar then made a series of changes aimed at transforming this space into a monumental appendage of his new Forum. Augustus continued this work of transformation by building the *Temple of Divus Iulius*; the new *Rostra ad Divi Iulii*, across from the former, embellished with the prows of the ships of Antony and Cleopatra; two arches commemorating the victories over the Parthians and Antony at Actium; and the *Portico of Gaius and Lucius Caesar*. Septimius Severus then added another arch at the beginning of the Via Sacra, opposite the Augustan Parthian Arch, which celebrated his victories over the Parthians. When the population of Rome began to grow and the emperors began building new

down from the Capitolium. The buildings have been described here beginning from the entrance to the archaeological zone. If you prefer to follow a chronological route through the monuments, you should begin from the *Regia*, proceed to the Temple of Vesta, the Juturna Fountain, the Temple of Castor and Pollux, the Lapis Niger, the Curia and the Basilica Aemilia.

cella was covered with slabs of marble, although only the structure in peperino remains today; unfortunately, in fact, as was common practice in medieval times, most of the material was removed and used to build other structures.

THE ROUND TEMPLE, KNOWN AS THE TEMPLE OF ROMULUS

Even today, access to the Temple of Romulus is still through a bronze gate that was originally framed by a marble cornice. It is above the street level revealed by 19th century excavations, which can be dated to the Augustan era, thus leaving the foundations of the edifice visible.

The structure that still stands before the House of the Vestals was long known to be a temple that Maxentius dedicated to his son Romulus. It is a circular green brick building with a cupola roof, preceded by a semicircular façade with four niches that originally held statues. The entry gate in bronze, preceded by two columns of porphyry, is original. To the right and left, cipolin columns frame two deep, symmetrical apses that lead to the central room through two doors at the end of the long sides. One of the most accredited theories, strongly supported by the evidence, holds that the main structure is the *Temple of Jupiter Stator*. The ancient cult of this deity was supposedly restored by Constantine, after Maxentius had dedicated the monument to Romulus for a brief time. The statues of the Penates, which in the 4th century AD had been moved from their original position, were placed here in the two side rooms.

THE BASILICA OF MAXENTIUS AND CONSTANTINE

In the early 4th century, Maxentius built a magnificent judicial basilica that held the prefecture, which from that time on became a single organ for the whole city administration. The structure replaced an earlier complex from the Flavian era, the *Horrea Piperataria*, which were warehouses for pepper, spices, herbs and medicines.

The building had a large central nave that ended in an apse to the west. It was covered by three immense cross vaults, supported by eight columns almost 15 meters in size. The two aisles were covered with barrel vaults and caisson ceilings. The first entrance was to the east and preceded by a horizontal vestibule, thus giving the monument an east-west orientation that was changed when it was completed by Constantine, who added a second entrance to the south onto the *Via Sacra*; here, a stairway led inside,

through a porticoed entry preceded by four Corinthian columns. Inside, on the opposite side, another apse was built, embellished by numerous statues; closed by a gate, it gave privacy to a new form of trial reserved for the senatorial class. The floor was embellished by geometrical designs made of different types of marbles. Slabs of marble covered the inside walls as well, making it appear truly magnificent and imposing. This image was also reinforced by the presence of the statue of the emperor Maxentius, which after his death was replaced with an enormous marble and bronze statue of Constantine located in the west apse. To get an idea of the size of the entire statue, look at what remains of it in the courtyard of the Palazzo dei Conservatori on the Capitoline Hill: the emperor's foot, which alone is 2 meters long, and his head.

THE FORUM OF AUGUSTUS

Augustus had decided to build a forum as early as 42 BC, following a vow he had made before the battle of Philippi against Brutus and Cassius, who murdered Caesar. Still, the work was not completed until 2 BC. Private parties purchased the land, while war booty was used to build it. The area he was able to utilize and expropriate from the landowners was not large. Built a little later than the Forum of

podium of the Temple dedicated to *Mars Ultor*, or the avenger. To the right and left of the temple were two large exedrae, inserted into the two-story arcade that surrounded the square on two sides. Niches carved into the two cipolin semicolumns held marble statues of historical and mythological persons: Aeneas with Anchises and Ascanius and the ancestors of the *gens Iulia* on one side, and Romulus with the *Summi Viri*, the great personages of the Republic, on the other.

Outside on the upper portion of the arcade were statues of caryatids (copies of those in the Erectheum of Athens), symbols of conquered nations, alternating with heads of

Jupiter Ammon. In the center of the space was the great statue of Augustus on his triumphal chariot. There was also an imposing statue of the emperor in the square room in back of the north portico. Here there were also two famous paintings by the painter Apelles, portraying Alexander the Great.

Nothing was left to chance in the iconography and organization of space. An expression of Augustan compromise, even the position of the statues revealed an effort to link Republican history with the history of the Julia family; within this framework, the empire fit perfectly as the supreme culmination of the Republic.

THE TEMPLE OF MARS ULTOR

To indicate a certain political continuity, the Temple of Mars occupied the same position as the Temple of Venus in the Forum of Caesar. A large central stairway with an altar in the center led to the podium. The cella was entered through a row of columns (eight in the front and a double row of eight on the sides). The interior had columns on two levels against the walls; there were niches between them for statues. In the back, in the apse, were the two religious statues of Mars and the goddess Venus. The famous Parthian Standards that Augustus took back

Caesar, it was meant to create a new space for trials and commercial affairs, but primarily exalted the figure of the emperor. The organization of space and the forum's decoration should be interpreted in this way, as a true political message, designed to transmit the image of Augustus as a conqueror and peacemaker who was respectful of *mos maiorum*, or ancient tradition.

A 33-meter-high wall of peperino and *lapis gabinus* completely surrounded the area, isolating it from the Subura district. Two flights of steps led down from this district and the forum area below and led to the two entrances to the Forum of Augustus, next to the

51 left Augustus began building his forum after 42 BC and the battle of Philippi against Brutus and Cassius, Caesar's murderers, but it was not completed until 2 BC. It has a central square surrounded by a high wall of peperino and lapis gabinus; the Temple of Mars Ultor was at the back, and to the right and left were two large exedrae in the two-story arcade.

51 right The Temple of Mars continued the tradition Caesar had begun with his Forum, as Augustus set himself to carry out the dictator's policies. The Temple dominated the Forum with its long stairway leading to the podium and the cella.

from the Parthians may also have been located here.

While the continuity of Roman tradition is evident, there is also a clear inspiration from the classical Greek world. We know that the Senate met here a number of times to make important decisions, such as whether to declare war or sanction a peace accord.

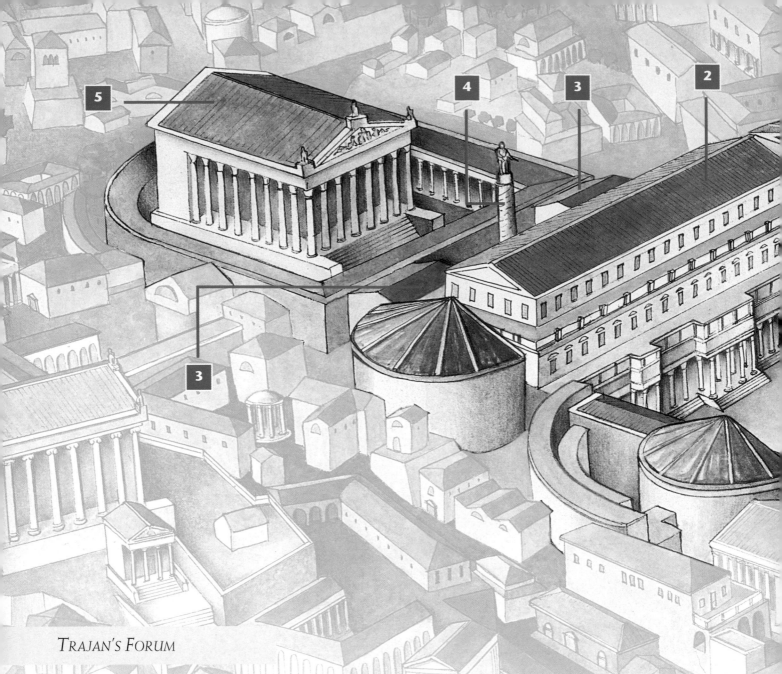

TRAJAN'S FORUM

Built between 107 (the year the Dacian wars ended in victory) and 113 AD, the great Forum of Trajan was the last of the great squares of the imperial epoch, designed to expand the civic and political center of the city of Rome. Over the centuries, the forum elicited the admiration of visitors due to its imposing size and the masterful compositional equilibrium, especially designed to become a homogenous complex by the famous imperial architect, Apollodorus of Damascus. He accomplished the great work of cutting the col that joined the Capitoline Hill to the Quirinal, without which there would have been no room to build it, given the density of buildings in that area. Even today, Trajan's Column is an extraordinary testimony to the original height of the col.

Overall, the complex was built using slightly raised terraces on which the monuments were placed. The square, about 300 meters long, was accessible from the Forum of Augustus through an arch with one fornix surmounted by an attic and flanked by walls dotted with semicolumns. On the two long sides was a colonnaded portico preceded by two flights of steps and embellished with statues of various personalities. On the high attic, sculptures of Dacian prisoners alternated with shields with heads. Behind the portico, one before the other, were two large semicircular exedrae, while in the center the equestrian statue of the emperor dominated the area. To the back, the view was blocked by the imposing façade of the *Basilica Ulpia*. Trajan clearly used the Forum of Augustus as

a model, thus presenting himself as continuing Augustus' political enterprises. The *Basilica Ulpia*, however, was somewhat of an innovation over previous models. The scheme used closely followed the emperor's militaristic policy: This included the arrangement of the buildings, which resembled the structure of military camps, with a square in the center (the forum's open area); a basilica (the *Basilica Ulpia*) next to the sanctuary of the legionary standards (Trajan's Column); and a place for the military archives (the two libraries). We know from various sources that the Forum served multiple functions. Laws were promulgated here, emperors bestowed so-called *congiaria*, monetary donations to the populace, and schools and reading areas were located here.

fill in the gap.

The remains now visible are for the most part from a restoration by Domitian.

Temple C, a *periptero sine postico*, was the oldest edifice, from the late 4th to the early 3rd century BC. It was probably a temple dedicated to Feronia. *Temple A*, the northernmost temple, followed immediately thereafter and can be dated to the mid-3rd century BC. The edifice, identified as the Temple of Juturna (another theory holds that it was dedicated to Juno *Curtis*), was probably built by Lutatius Catulus after the battle against the Carthaginians, and later underwent

some radical changes. As it currently appears, it is a peripteral hexastyle, with fluted tufa columns and travertine Corinthian capitals.

Temple D, the largest of the four temples, is dated to the early 2nd century BC, and stands on the far east side of the area. It has been hypothesized that it is the Temple of the Lares Permarini, but this theory is still questioned. The current structure, entirely in travertine, is from a late Republican remodeling.

The last in time is *Temple B*. It is a circular edifice with a flight of stairs leading to the podium. The Corinthian columns are in tufa, while the bases and capitals are in travertine. It is almost certainly the Temple of *Fortuna Huiusce Diei* ("of that day"), dedicated by another Lutatius Catulus following the battle of Vercelli against the Cimbri.

THE THEATER OF BALBUS

The Theater of Balbus (about 11,000 spectators), was the smallest of the three theaters on the *Campus Martius*. It was dedicated by Cornelius Balbus, a Roman banker friend of Augustus, in 13 BC but, on the day it was opened, the Tiber flooded and the theater could only be reached by boat. Its remains were found beneath the Palazzo Mattei-Paganica. Behind the scene was a large rectangular area known as the *Crypta Balbi*, surrounded by a portico with pillars and completed by a large exedra. From a funeral inscription, we know that the portico was used for commercial activities, such as the sale of high-quality bronzes. In the Middle Ages, the crypt was used by ropemakers, hence the name to the nearby church of Santa Caterina dei Funari (from the Latin *funis*).

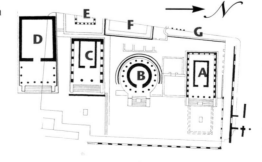

PLAN OF THE LARGO ARGENTINA SACRED AREA
A. TEMPLE OF JUTURNA
B. TEMPLE OF FORTUNA HUIUSCE DIEI
C. TEMPLE OF FERONIA
D. TEMPLE OF LARES PERMARINI
E. PUBLIC LATRINE
F. CURIA OF THE PORTICOES OF POMPEY
G. LATRINE

THE THEATER AND PORTICO OF POMPEY

The Theater of Pompey was the first permanent theater of the city of Rome. Work on this complex began around 61 BC, on land that probably already belonged to C. Pompey. In 55 BC, the year of the second consulate of Pompey,

great games were organized to celebrate the opening. The cavea was 150 meters in diameter and could hold up to 18,000 spectators. On the top (*summa cavea*) was a *temple of Victory*. Temple buildings and performance structures were often associated in the Roman world. Behind the scene was a large portico (180x135), which Atticus, Cicero's friend, embellished with statues of the most famous Greek artists, depicting subjects related to the world of theater or to Venus. There were works of art on the scene as well, some of which have been found (two large sculptures are now at the Louvre). In the center of the portico were two groves of plane trees with fountains.

On the opposite side, behind the circular temple on Largo Argentina, there was a large rectangular exedra, a *Curia* used for Senate meetings, decorated with a statue of Pompey. It was here that Julius Caesar was assassinated in 44 BC. After the murder, the *Curia* was walled up (32 BC) and later transformed into a latrine. The theater survived over the centuries, and in fact the houses that were built in this area followed its inner curve exactly (Piazza di Grotta Pinta). For example, Palazzo Righetti stands where the Temple of *Venus Victrix* was located.

AGRIPPA'S BATHS

Agrippa's Baths were the most ancient public baths of Rome. They were originally private baths that were only donated to the Roman populace later, through a will. They were built by Agrippa, Augustus' son-in-law, between 25 and 19 BC, between the Pantheon and the Theater of Pompey, north of the Largo Argentina area (the present-day Via di Santa Chiara and Corso Vittorio Emanuele). The facilities, which extended over a surface area 120 x 80/100 meters in size, had the traditional structure of the most ancient baths, with rooms placed irregularly around a circular central room, 25 meters in diameter. We know that the baths were embellished by numerous works of art by famous Greek artists, such as the

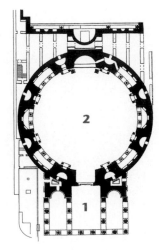

1. PRONAOS
2. CELLA

64 right top The Pantheon consists of a deep pronaos, divided horizontally into three naves, and a large circular cella, into which are carved numerous niches and circular and rectangular openings.

THE PANTHEON

With Hadrian, there was a return to classicism, which had once also characterized Augustan political and artistic decisions. Here, however, the style is new, more eclectic, and tends to blend Greek and Roman models. Considered the emperor of consolidation more than of expansion, Hadrian's political orientation was also reflected in his artistic decisions, which he followed personally with great interest. This was also part of an attempt to seek a common identity for all regions of the empire, with the goal of holding it together in this way. And

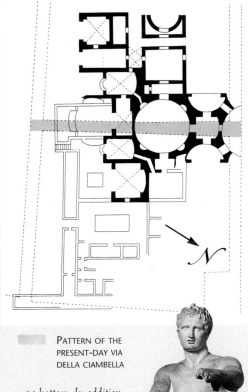

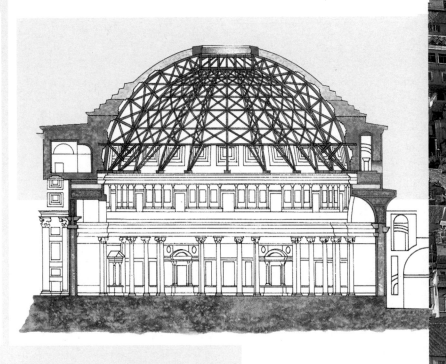

PATTERN OF THE PRESENT-DAY VIA DELLA CIAMBELLA

64 bottom In addition to the numerous porticoes, beautiful statues by Greek artists or replicas of the famous originals adorned thermal edifices as well. The subjects of these works of art often used bath motifs, like the Apoxyomenos by Lysippus, of an athlete cleaning himself.

famous statue of *Apokyomenos* by Lysippus (an athlete scraping himself with a strigil), a 50 AD replica of which fortunately remains. To the west was the *Stagnum Agrippae*, a man-made lake that was probably used as a swimming pool for the baths and was fed by the *Virgo* aqueduct. Overall, it was a large recreational complex that completed the performance district. Today, the only portion remaining is the masonry structure of the circular hall from a Severian-era remodeling, over which the Via dell'Arco della Ciambella now runs (nos.9 and 15).

64 center right and bottom The Pantheon structure is quite complex and could be termed "self-supporting." The cylinder at the base consists of 16 niches carved into the walls. The empty spaces thus radially formed act as supporting pillars, connected by safety arches. The cupola is placed about halfway up and includes a reinforcement ring that contains the oblique pressure of the vault. The lacunars that decorate the vault also help lighten the weight, as does the use of increasingly lightweight materials (such as layers of concrete alternating with tufa and volcanic slag for the upper portion).

of the stairway that led to the podium. Some remains are still visible below the church, near the apse. Very probably the temple was dedicated to Juno Sospita, Juno protectress of births.

THE NORTHERN TEMPLE. The Ionic temple to the north is the best preserved. It is located to the right of S. Nicola in Carcere. It was a peripteral hexastyle building *sine postico*, with a triple row of columns on the façade and a colonnade on the long sides (two columns remain on one side and seven

on the other; they were about 26 x 15 meters in size). It stood on a podium covered with blocks of travertine, preceded by a stairway. The temple was presumably dedicated to Janus, and according to sources was located *iuxta Theatrum Marcelli*, that is, near the Theater of Marcellus. Built in the Republican period, during the First Punic War, by Duilius, the winner of the battle of Mylae, it was rebuilt a number of times until the time of Hadrian.

76 right Three temples from the Republican era stand within the church of San Nicola in Carcere. The southern temple is smaller and more ancient, and was probably dedicated to Spes. The central temple, which may have been built last, was consecrated to Juno Sospita (in the photo), and finally, the Ionic, peripteral, hexastyle temple to the north was dedicated to Janus.

77 top left On the Piazza di San Giorgio in Velabro is an arch (which was most probably an entry gate to the forum) decorated with splendid relief work. It was built in 203 AD by cattle merchants and silversmiths, the bankers of the time, in honor of Septimius Severus.

77 bottom Elaborate vegetal decoration almost completely covers the Arco degli Argentari. There is a frieze in the lower portion of the pillars depicting the sacrifice of bulls. Above, to the left, is a larger scene, probably portraying Caracalla. On the outer portion of the arch, in the photo, are military soldiers leading a barbarian prisoner.

77 top right Near the descent of the Velabrum is a large four-faced arch known as the Arch of Janus. It was built around the 4th century AD by Constantius II, in honor of the emperor Constantine.

THE ARCO DEGLI ARGENTARI

In 203 AD, livestock merchants and bankers, known as *argentarii*, built an arch in honor of Septimius Severus on Piazza San Giorgio al Velabro. More than an arch, it was probably a monumental gate leading into the *Forum Boarium*. Almost seven meters high, it has two masonry pillars with a marble architrave, where the statues were originally located. The pillars were decorated with sculpted panels, framed by pilasters with military standards and volutes of acanthus. Between the pillars one can see friezes with Victories and eagles, the sacrifice of a bull in the lower section, and a depiction of sacrificial tools on the upper section. The largest panels show a standing male figure that can be identified as the emperor Caracalla, two soldiers with a barbarian, and Caracalla once again, preparing a libation. Next to

him, in an empty space, must have been the figure of Geta, which was later removed. Inside the arch, Septimius Severus is depicted with his wife Julia Domna; on the architrave is Hercules with the lion skin and club, and next to him the figure of a Genius.

THE FOUR-FACED ARCH OF JANUS

At the feet of the descent of the Velabrum is a large monument, a four-faced arch known as the Arch of Janus, dating to the 4th century AD and built in honor of the emperor Constantine. It had four pillars covered in marble that supported a cross vault. On the outside, two rows of three niches ending in hemispherical shell calottes were used to hold statues. The four keystones of the arches are sculpted with figures of Rome and Juno, seated, and Minerva and Ceres, standing. The attic, now lost, must have been located above. Fragments of the inscription have been preserved in the nearby church of San Giorgio in Velabro.

According to legend, after the Tarquinians were driven from Rome, the grain of the *Campus Martius*, land that was once owned by the Etruscan kings, was cut and thrown into the river. This supposedly created Tiber Island (the Isola Tiberina), although it is now believed to date back to a much earlier period. Another legend states that due to a terrible pestilence, a delegation was sent to the temple of Aesculapius (the god of medicine) in Epidaurus. The delegation returned to Rome with a

porticos used to house the ill. The island was long a place for healing, and even today the hospital Fatebenefratelli, dating back to 1548, is located here.

There were two ways to get to the island, the *Pons Fabricius* (Fabricius Bridge) that connected it to the *Campus Martius*, and the *Pons Cestius* (Cestius Bridge) to Transtiberim. Originally, a ferry or wooden barge was probably used to cross the river.

The *Pons Fabricius* was built in 62 BC by Lucius Fabricius, as the inscription

states. It was 62 meters long and had two large arches resting on a central pier, within which was a small arch, useful for lowering water pressure in the case of floods.

The *Pons Cestius*, built in 46 BC, was originally about 50 meters long and had a large central archway and two smaller ones on the sides; it was completely rebuilt in the 1800s. The inscription that commemorates a remodeling in the 4th century AD is located in the center of one of the bridge's abutments.

serpent, symbol of the god, which when set free supposedly jumped into the Tiber and swam to the island, thus indicating the place where a temple dedicated to Aesculapius should be built. The present-day *Church of San Bartolomeo* stands right on the spot of the ancient *Temple of Aesculapius*, of which no trace remains, except perhaps the medieval well in the center of the stairs, which could be the primitive sacred font, just as the 14 columns within the church may belong to the temple. Within the sanctuary, like that at Epidaurus, there must have been

78 Isola Tiberina is in the middle of a bend in the Tiber, in an area of great historical significance. This had been an almost mandatory river crossing from the very earliest times, and thus controlling it was originally of crucial importance.

79 left The Pons Fabricius, built in 62 BC, was 62 meters long. It still has the two large spans resting on the central pier, where there was a small arch that helped decrease water pressure in the event of flooding.

90 bottom An older floor, with colored marble decorations, was found below the triclinium of the Domus Flavia. It must have been part of an edifice on top of which Domitian built his palace, perhaps Nero's Domus.

91 top To the southwest was a large banquet hall facing two elliptical nymphaea, of which the western one has been preserved; its fountains impressed guests at opulent official dinners.

91 bottom In the center of the Domus Flavia is a vast rectangular peristyle surrounded by a colonnaded portico. In the center, we can still see the remains of the octagonal fountain, with low walls arranged to form a labyrinth.

92 top left The complex's structures were originally covered in marble. The decoration was also sumptuous, due to the numerous works of

art that made the place even more pleasant.

92 top right The Stadium, fully 160 meters long with one of the short sides

curved, was surrounded by a portico with pillars on two levels. It was used not so much for spectacles and games as for walks and horseback rides.

92 center The remains of a Republican house were found below the Domus Flavia, at the level of the Basilica. One of the rooms is frescoed with late style II

architectural-type paintings. The decorations on the ceiling, with interwining ribbons that frame scenes with symbols of Isis, gave the place its name.

Under the Basilica, in an area not open to the public, were found the remains of a rich Republican house. A large rectangular space revealed advanced style II frescoes datable to the mid-first century BC, now on exhibit at the Loggia Mattei. The decorative scheme is of a traditional architectural type, while the decoration of the vault, which has given this hall its name, is particularly original. It consists of two ribbons, one red and one blue, that interweave in a complicated pattern and frame scenes with symbols of Isis and objects sacred to her cult (lotus flowers, garlands of roses, and asps). This type of decoration became fashionable at the time of Augustus after the battle of Actium, when it was used in dwellings for its ornamental value, with no special religious significance.

92 bottom The Stadium is on the eastern side of the complex of Domitian palaces. Halfway down the east side is a large exedra that was originally surrounded by a corridor on two levels; this was the imperial family's box.

100-101 In the 2nd century BC, Rome had to build a new river port in the only area still available, at the foot of the Aventine, the so-called Emporium. The area was thus paved, and wharves and barriers, steps leading down to the river, and the dock were built. The side of the dock facing the Tiber has large blocks of travertine with rings used to moor the boats.

imposing *Porticus Aemilia*, a storehouse for incoming materials, made of tufa in *opus incertum*, by Lucius Aemilius Lepidus and Lucius Aemilius Paulus. The complex was almost 500 meters long. It was divided into 50 aisles by pillars (seven deep) and was covered by a series of small vaults jutting out one over the other. Some parts of the walls are still visible between vie Branca and Vespucci.

When Rome's population began to increase in the 2nd century BC, free distributions of grain to the populace also increased, and as a consequence more space was needed. There were many of these food warehouses, or *Horrea*, between *Porticus Aemilia* and Mount Testaccio. The best known were the *Horrea Galbana*, which consisted of three buildings with a central courtyard and a series of rooms all around. Recently, however, these areas have also been identified as the dwellings of the numerous slaves employed here.

THE TESTACCIO

few rooms of a *Mithraeum* have also been found over these structures.

The *Mithraeum* of Santa Prisca, from the 2nd century AD and destroyed in the 1400s, is accessible through the church's left aisle. Through a crypt, you reach a *spaeleum*, preceded by an atrium. Near the entrance, two niches were used for statues of Mithras' helpers, *Cautes* and *Cautopates*; in the back was another niche showing a rather common scene of Mithras killing a bull, with a reclining Saturn visible below; both figures are made of amphorae covered in stucco. On the side walls are paintings of people in procession carrying objects/symbols of the various levels of their initiation: the crow, the *nymphus*, the soldier, the lion, the Persian, the *Heliodromos*, the father.

The remains of another thermal facility, the *Decian Baths*, built by the

emperor Decius in 252 AD, were found below the square of the Temple of Diana. The plan has survived due to a design by Palladio.

Beginning in the 2nd century BC, the cattle market was no longer large enough to meet the needs of trade, which required more and more practical features and space for commodities, and housing for the multitudes employed in the various operations. Thus, a new river port was built in a still-vacant area at the foot of the Aventine, the so-called *Emporium*. The paving was completed, and barriers, wharves and stairways descending to the Tiber were built, along with a pier fully 500 meters long, in front of which were large blocks of travertine with mooring rings for the ships.

In the area behind it were numerous service buildings like the

The *Testaccio* — the hill of potsherds — is an artificial rise on the left bank of the Tiber, between the Aurelian Walls and the present-day Via Galvani. It is about 30 meters above street level and has a total surface area of about 20,000 square meters.

The present-day name comes from the Latin *testa*, which means shard. It was here, in fact, that broken amphorae were customarily tossed after being unloaded from ships moored at the nearby port. Most were oil amphorae of the "Dressel 20" type, bearing the factory mark on the handles and an indication of origin and the various controls on the body. The majority of the containers came from Spain, especially Betica, the present-day Andalusia, while others came from North Africa. Most of the amphorae can be dated to a period between the mid-2nd and the mid-3rd century AD.

THE PYRAMID OF CAIUS CESTIUS

C(aius) Cestius L(uci) f(ilius) Epulo, Pob(lilia tribu), praetor, tribunus plebis, (septem)vir epulonum

"Caius Cestius Epulus, son of Lucius, of the Poblilia tribe, praetorian, tribune of the plebeians, septemvirate responsible for the sacred banquets "

This inscription comes from a pyramid-shaped monument that can still be seen on Piazza Ostiense. Added to the Aurelian Walls in the 3rd century, in the Middle Ages it was known as the *Meta Remi*; it is a funeral monument built for Cestius. On the bases of the bronze statues of the deceased, now in the Musei Capitolini, were other inscriptions that named the illustrious heirs, including Valerius Messalla and Agrippa, Augustus' son-in-law. We know that these statues were made with money from *attalica*, i.e. precious vellum tapestries, which could not be placed inside due to a recent law (18 BC) against extravagance. The pyramid was originally surrounded by four columns, and was based on models from Ptolemaic Egypt, like the pyramids of Meröe. The monument, made in *opus caementicium*, is covered in marble slabs. It was almost 30 meters at the base and was 36.40 meters high. The inner chamber, accessible through a modern entrance, was rectangular and had a barrel vault. The brick facing is one of the oldest examples of this type of technique (*opus latericium*) that has survived to this day. The style three pictorial decoration was especially rich, featuring panels framed by candelabras with seated and standing female figures in the center. There were four Victories at the four corners of the vault.

102 *An imposing pyramid stands on Piazza Ostiense — the burial monument of Caius Cestius. In the Middle Ages it was known as the* Meta Remi, *and was related to another structure, the* so-called Meta Romuli. *The statue of the deceased that stood here is now on view at the Capitoline Museums. The original pyramid of Cestius was to be surrounded by columns; the architect* certainly modeled his work after pyramids in Ptolemaic Egypt. The outer surface of the monument is covered with sheets of marble, while the structure itself is in opus caementicium.

TRASTEVERE

The Trastevere was the last of the 14 Augustan regions and included, in addition to Isola Tiberina, the right bank of the river to the Janiculum hill. Originally, however, the Trastevere was outside the urban area (separated by the *Pomoerium* until the time of Vespasian), but had nevertheless been an extremely important area ever since the age of the kings.

The Janiculum hills were a natural bulwark against Etruria, and thus indispensable for Rome's defense. Tradition states that a red flag was raised here when *Comitia* were held in the *Campus Martius*. When, during the Republican era, the new port was built (in the present-day Testaccio quarter),

were in charge of supervising two of the Augustan regions (IX and XIV).

The working-class nature of the quarter can also be seen in the cults that arose here. There was a large Jewish community in this area, and it appears that the ancient synagogue stood near the present-day Porta Portese. There were also numerous temples dedicated to the *Goddess Dia*, *Fors Fortuna* (three of them, two on Via Portuense) and the *Divae Corniscae*. Several more of these religious buildings have also been found in the area of Porta Portese, Viale Trastevere, and near the Ministry of Public Education. There was also a large number of sanctuaries for

Oriental cults that served as meeting places for foreign communities and new Roman followers. They included an important *Syriac sanctuary* discovered on the Janiculum.

THE JANICULUM

On the southern slopes of the Janiculum, as early as the 2nd century BC, there was a religious edifice dedicated to *Zeus Keraunios* and the Furies. Around the first century AD, this cult was connected to the Syriac deities, for whom a sanctuary was built (the present-day remains, however, date back to a 4th century AD reconstruction). It has a rather elongated plan in three sections. The entrance, halfway down one of the long sides, led to a large rectangular courtyard. This led into two other rooms: To the left was an atrium with two side cellae; through them one reached a basilica-type hall with a nave and two aisles, with a triangular altar in the center and at the back a large apse, for the main religious statue, in the form of a seated Jupiter. To the right, two doors led to another quite original room with a mixtilinear plan. It consisted of two smaller rooms at the sides and a larger one, with a more or less octagonal shape, with an apse at the back. Here as well, a triangular altar was found at the center, in a cavity in which several eggs and a small bronze statue were found. This *simulacrum* depicted a

PLAN OF THE EXCUBITORIUM OF THE 7TH COHORT

A. CHAPEL (LARARIUM) DEDICATED TO THE GENIUS OF THE BARRACKS
B. BASIN OF FOUNTAIN
C. EXEDRA
D. GUARDS' LODGINGS

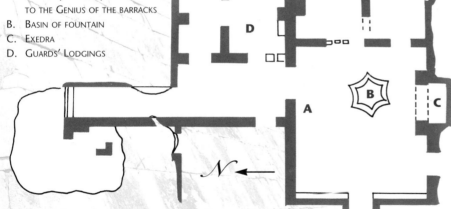

the area began to fill with service buildings and the dwellings of port workers and merchants. This was accentuated during the imperial period, when artisans, potters, millers, porters and workers, along with a large number of immigrants from the Orient, chose this place for their homes. Below the *church of Santa Cecilia* (Via della Lungaretta), at the level of the nave, structures have been found from Republican-era *horrea* and a hide-tanning workshop from the Antonine age, identified through the presence of seven hemispherical vats.

On Viale Trastevere, between Via Montefiore and Via della VII Coorte, eight meters below street level, is the *Excubitorium of the VII cohort of guards*, the barracks used for the guards who, like modern policemen and firefighters,

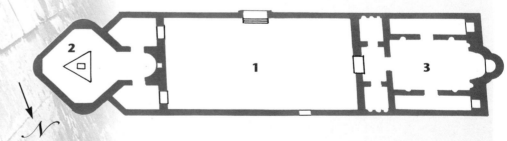

PLAN OF THE SANCTUARY TO ISIS
1. RECTANGULAR COURTYARD
2. MIXTILINEAR AREA WITH APSE
3. BASILICA STRUCTURE

male figure wrapped in the coils of a snake, and represented the god Osiris, who was buried each year to be reborn again through seven celestial spheres (the seven coils of the serpent), symbolizing the initiation of the faithful.

115 top left While the
bath ritual was more or
less rigidly established,
the physical exercises
that preceded it and took
place within the
palaestra were not, and
were left to the
individual visitor,
who could test his or
her mettle in wrestling,
boxing, weightlifting,
running or fencing.
Women devoted
themselves primarily
to games with the
ball and hoop,
although some
preferred more
"masculine" exercises
such as weightlifting.

covered by a high cupola in which
there were numerous windows that used
the sun as a further source of heat. Then
came a cold bath to reactivate the
circulation. In baths that did not have a
special *frigidarium* for this, tubs of cold
water were placed in the exedrae of the
basilica hall. The basilica was in the
center of the complex, and thus also
acted as a link, reception area and
meeting place, and also resolved the
difficult problem of practicability of the
facilities, which could be frequented by
as many as 3000 people at a time, as
were the Diocletian Baths. The itinerary
ended with a bath in the *natatio*, the
swimming pool, and massages and body
oils that protected the body from the
change in outside temperature.

It was a real problem to heat and
supply the enormous quantity of water
needed for the myriad thermal facilities

in Rome (it has been estimated that
there were about 1000 of them in the
4th century AD). Until the first century
BC, an outside furnace and stoves for
the inside were the most common
solution.

In 89 BC, a new, quite practical
system was developed, known as the
Hypocaust. It consisted of parallel rows
of brick pillars arranged in
checkerboard fashion, resting on an
underpavement of tiles or large bricks,
tilted toward the source of heat (an
expedient that served to obtain a better
diffusion of heat). Above, there were
large, so-called "two-footed" bricks, on
which rested a layer of cocciopesto; the
floor itself followed. For the side walls,
hollow spaces were inserted with *tegulae
mammatae* followed by rectangular,
hollow bricks, which connected to the
loose stone foundation below.

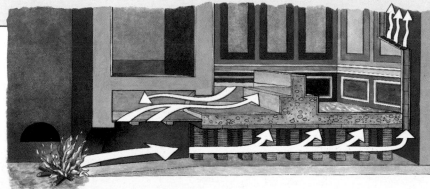

115 top right and center
The great social and
political role played by
thermal baths, which
could be termed true
"people's villas," fully
justifies the great efforts
of engineers and
architects to find
increasingly innovative
technical solutions that
were grandiose but at the
same time practical (such
as, for example, the use of
adequate materials).

115 bottom The
system for heating the
thermal areas included
the use of
suspensurae, air
spaces located below
the pavement,
supported by small
pillars (often behind
the walls as well,
through small tubes),
which helped diffuse
warm air from the
boiler, the
prefurnius.

114 bottom The rich
decoration inside
Caracalla's Baths that
must have made this
complex especially
pleasant for visitors,
unfortunately has not
survived. The few remains
of sculptures have been
transferred to the large
national museums, as have
the mosaics. Only
architectural elements
remain in situ, such as
marble capitals and parts of
columns, providing a pale
reflection of the sumptuous
original decoration.

THE VIA APPIA

The *Via Appia* began at the *Circus Maximus*, near the present-day Piazza di Porta Capena, ran past Caracalla's Baths and crossed the *Via Latina*. As the law forbade burying the dead within the city walls, as the centuries passed, the roads that branched off from the center gradually assumed a strong funerary nature, due to the succession of monuments in various sizes and shapes. Large funeral processions left for the cremation pyre built outside the walls. If the deceased was a patrician, not only did surviving relatives participate in these processions, but so did the ancestors (played by actors wearing masks that resembled the ancestors). Following were men carrying images of what the deceased had done in his lifetime, and finally the Dead himself, his face uncovered, carried in a litter. Not only was it a sacred obligation to bury the dead, but there was also a strong need to keep the memory of the deceased alive by building grandiose

116 left The *Via Appia* was one of the most important roads in Rome. From Porta Capena, Roman proconsuls departed for their assigned provinces, and magistrates and emperors left and returned from here. The road was thus equipped with official structures related to this function, such as the building where the Senate conferred with generals on their return from the provinces, the Mutatorium Caesaris, where the emperor changed his clothing, and the Temple of the God Rediculus.

VIA APPIA

1. PORTA APPIA (PORTA S. SEBASTIANO)
2. SO-CALLED TOMB OF GETA
3. COLOMBARIUM OF AUGUSTUS' FREEDMEN
4. COLOMBARIUM OF LIVIA'S FREEDMEN
5. TOMB OF THE VOLUSII'S FREEDMEN
6. CATACOMBS OF ST. CALLISTO
7. CATACOMBS OF DOMITILLA
8. CATACOMBS OF ST. SEBASTIAN AND CHURCH OF ST. SEBASTIAN
9. VILLA AND CIRCUS OF MAXENTIUS
10. MAUSOLEUM OF MAXENTIUS
11. MAUSOLEUM OF CAECILIA METELLA
12. MAUSOLEUM WITH PYRAMID
13. VILLA OF THE QUINTILII
14. CASAL ROTONDO

116 bottom right There were various types of tombs located along the Via Appia; some looked like houses, with painted decorations, some like tumuli, pyramids, little temples or shrines. Marble relief work decorated the monuments, often with portraits of the deceased.

116-117 Beyond the Porta di San Sebastiano in the Aurelian Walls, the suburban portion of the Via Appia began. We know that in ancient times it was rather monumental in appearance, due to the succession of tombs of various sizes and shapes. According to law, in fact, except in special cases, the dead could only be buried outside the city walls.

structures where a large number of people could see them: along the roads. The family tombs, like that of the *Scipii*, in the Republican era, sometimes looked like actual houses with painted decorations. But they could also take on a different form, like a *tumulus* or a *pyramid*. Even the less well-to-do, while still alive, could ensure themselves a place in a large collective tomb, within whose walls were carved countless niches to hold urns, thus giving them the name of *colombarii* (dovecotes).

117 top Yesterday as today, there was a strong need to keep the memory of the dead alive, including through architectural works that held their remains, adorned with relief work and statues placed where a large number of people could see them – along the roads.

117 center The Tomb of Annia Regilla, also known as the Temple of the God Rediculus, is actually a two-story patrician tomb from the early 2nd century. The burial chamber was on the lower level, while the upper portion was used for religious purposes.

117 bottom The so-called Casal Rotondo, near the great Villa of the Quintilii, is the largest circular tomb on the Via Appia, and is similar to the Tomb of Caecilia Metella.

126 top *Beginning in the 11th century, the name* Coliseum *was popularly adopted to indicate the amphitheater. It comes from Nero's* Colossus, *which stood a short distance away. Begun by Vespasian, it was completed by Titus in 80 AD. Games of various types were held here, such as hunts and gladiator combat.*

126-127 *The Coliseum has an oval design; the various orders of bleachers are supported by a complex series of superimposed walls. On the outside, we can still see four superimposed architectural orders on the north side, done in* opus quadratum *in travertine, with the arcades framed by Tuscan, Ionic and Corinthian engaged columns. Shields and windows alternate on the fourth order.*

THE EXTERIOR. The amphitheater is oval in form, 188 meters long at its longest point and 156 meters at its shortest. Total height is 52 meters, divided into four stories of architectural orders, in travertine *opus quadratum*. The full elevation of the outside ring has survived only on the northern side. The first three orders had 80 arches framed by Tuscan engaged columns on the first order, Ionic columns on the second, and Corinthian columns on the third; the fourth order was formed by 80 panels dotted with Corinthian pilasters, with alternating windows and *clipea* (round copper shields); there were three brackets in each square, corresponding to an equal number of openings in the cornice above, used to hold the wooden beams to which the *velarium* was attached. The *velarium* was a large linen awning used to protect spectators from the sun and rain; it was maneuvered by a special corps of sailors from the fleet of Misenum.

Entrances were marked by numbers carved over the arches, which corresponded to numbers marked on the tickets. In fact, despite the fact that these public spectacles were free, to attend, one had to have a token indicating an assigned seat and the way to get there.

127 bottom *The Amphitheater of Statilius Taurus originally stood in the valley between the Esquiline and the Velia. This edifice was destroyed in a fire, and Nero built a small lake in its place. Only during the time of Flavius did Rome finally receive an amphitheater worthy of the capital of such a large empire: the Flavian Amphitheater.*

128-129 The amphitheater's cavea was impressively large. The four sectors that seated the populace, from richest to poorest, depending on class, were located here in horizontal succession. To protect the spectators from the sun and rain, the velarium was unfolded above them. Its mechanism was set into brackets on the outer façade.

128 bottom The Coliseum's bleachers were divided into four sectors, where the populace was seated according to social station. Seating was rigidly preestablished.

129 top left On the last ring of the cavea were the wooden beams to which the velarium was attached. This was a large cover made of linen that protected spectators from summer heat and rain. A special corps of sailors from the fleet of Misenum was in charge of maneuvering the velarium.

129 top right Two underground corridors divided the Coliseum arena into four sections. The central corridor, which followed the major axis, continued below the steps at the east entry to reach the

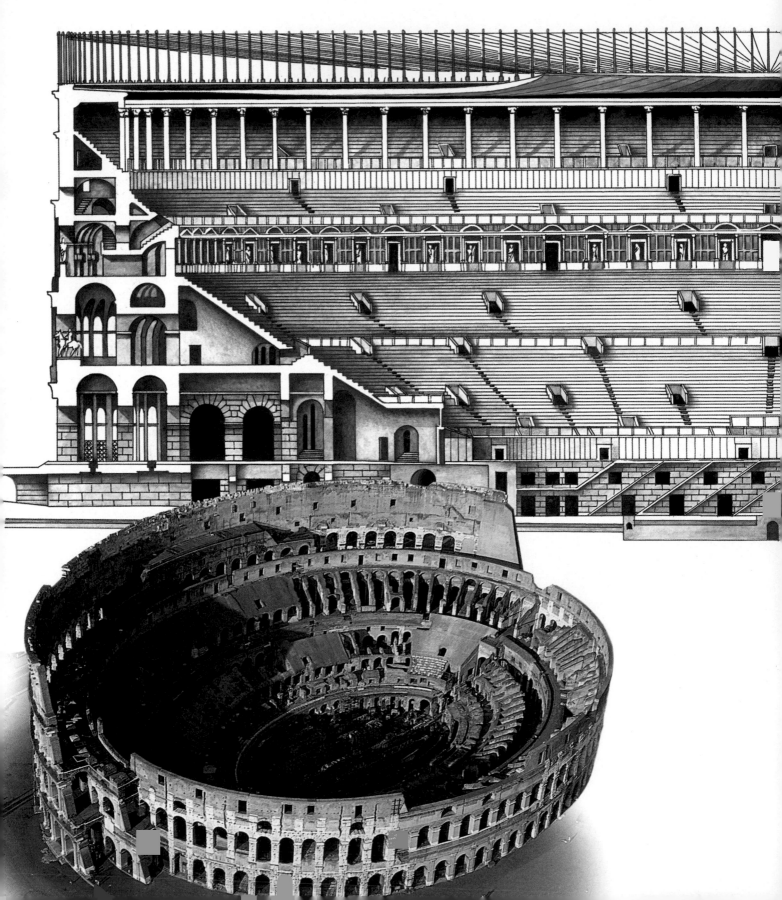

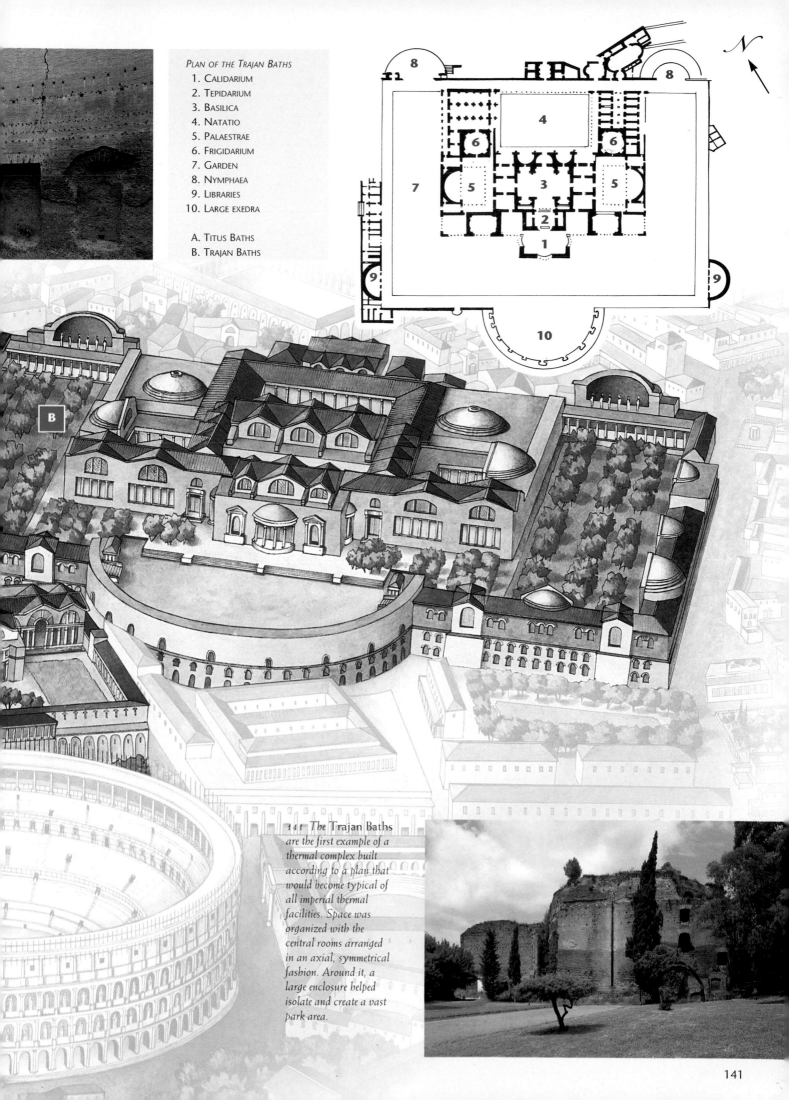

PLAN OF THE TRAJAN BATHS

1. CALIDARIUM
2. TEPIDARIUM
3. BASILICA
4. NATATIO
5. PALAESTRAE
6. FRIGIDARIUM
7. GARDEN
8. NYMPHAEA
9. LIBRARIES
10. LARGE EXEDRA

A. TITUS BATHS
B. TRAJAN BATHS

*141 The Trajan Baths
are the first example of a
thermal complex built
according to a plan that
would become typical of
all imperial thermal
facilities. Space was
organized with the
central rooms arranged
in an axial, symmetrical
fashion. Around it, a
large enclosure helped
isolate and create a vast
park area.*

142 left On Via San Vito, we can still see one of the three fornices of the Arch of Gallienus. It was originally the Esquiline Gate of the Servian Walls, completely rebuilt by Augustus and then rededicated by Marcus Aurelius Victor in the 3rd century AD, in honor of Gallienus.

The remains of the *Arch of Gallienus*, incorporated within the Servian Walls, can be seen on Via S. Vito, near Santa Maria Maggiore. The arch has been identified as one of the entry gates in the first walls of Rome, the antique-era *Porta Esquilina*. It was a gate with three entries, with the largest one in the center, and angular Corinthian pillars. The arch was completely rebuilt by Augustus.

142-143 The so-called Temple of Minerva stands majestically on Via Giolitti. It is actually a magnificent nymphaeum that

was part of the imperial villa of the Licinii, the Horti Licianiani. It was built in the 4th century in opus caementicium.

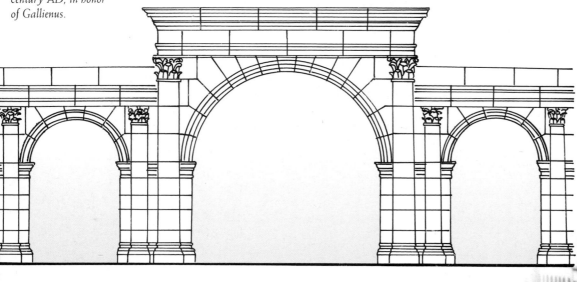

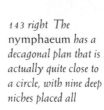

THE BASILICA OF JUNIUS BASSUS   THE TROPHIES OF MARIUS

Near the church of Santa Maria Maggiore, on Via Napoleone III 3, are the remains of a large aristocratic residence from the late antique period that probably belonged to Junius Bassus, who was consul in 331 BC. A state hall with an apse can be identified, preceded by a forked atrium, with a splendid *opus sextile* decoration (a decorative technique that used colored marble, ivory and vitreous paste intarsia), now on display at the Palazzo Massimo alle Terme. Two panels depicting the kidnapping of Hylas by nymphs, and a high-ranking person on a *quadriga*, probably Junius Brutus himself, are particularly beautiful. These mosaics clearly show how aristocratic Roman society, not yet converted to Christianity, used symbols to express ideological meanings, still keeping Pagan beliefs alive in the 4th century.

On the north side of Piazza Vittorio Emanuele, a green brick structure can be seen that has been known as the *Trophies of Marius* ever since Renaissance times. It was a monumental public fountain, probably supplied by a branch of the *Aqua Claudia* or the *Anio Novus*. The *nymphaeum*, completely covered in marble, was built by the emperor Alexandrus Severus (it is in fact known as the *Nymphaeum Alexandri*) before 226 AD. It has a trapezoidal plan on three floors decorated with numerous sculptures. Below, a large basin collected water that ran down from the upper level, and above was the monumental façade with an apse in the center and two arches at the sides. The marble trophies that were originally placed here were two reliefs from the Domitian era that were reused in the monument and later removed (they can now be admired on the balustrade of the Capitol).

143 right The nymphaeum has a decagonal plan that is actually quite close to a circle, with nine deep niches placed all

around it, except for the side with the entrance. There are nine large windows, above which was the circular cupola.

154 top The famous Canopus complex occupied a narrow depression that was supported by a series of buttresses and substructures. In the center is a long canal, while in the back is a temple-nymphaeum known as the Serapeum that had a semicircular exedra and was used as a cenatium.

Hadrian's Villa

155 center The canal, 119 meters long and 18 meters wide, ends to the north with a curved side (in the photograph) and has a colonnade with a mixtilinear architrave.

Two colonnades run along the long sides of the Canopus. The eastern one was double, while the western one was simple. Statues were located around the canal. Still remaining is the one depicting the Nile and a crocodile, reflecting the Egyptian theme of the entire complex. Within the basin were the bases that supported the Scylla groups, of which fragments have been found.

155 top left Statues of mythological characters, mirrored in the waters of the canal, stood between the columns that surrounded the Canopus. The only ones surviving are those of Ares, Athena, Hermes and two Amazons.

155 top right Along the west side of the Canopus, the columns are replaced by statues of six caryatids, two of whom depict Silenus, while the other four are replicas of those of the Erectheum at the Acropolis in Athens.

154 bottom and 155 bottom right The villa was richly decorated. Polychrome mosaics embellished the state rooms, often with emblems in the center that had an almost pictorial chiaroscuro effect, due to the use of very small tesserae. The works of art also included statues by famous artists done in precious marble, such as the Drunken Faun in red pavonazzetto marble, now at the Palazzo dei Conservatori.

the villa's main vestibule may have been here. Crossing over to the end of the terrace, we come to the Temple of Venus. This is a small, circular temple within a large semicircular exedra, with Doric columns. The model for the edifice came directly from the temple of Cnidus, where ancient writers tell us the famous statue of Aphrodite by Praxiteles was located; a copy is found here. Beyond the road are the remains of the small Greek Theater, which must have been used for performances for the court (it held only 500 spectators). A portion of the cavea remains, up against the slope, from which one could see the stage along with the lovely background of hills.

OSTIA

While sources agree that primitive Ostia was founded in the age of Ancus Marcius in the 7th century BC, when Rome was expanding to the Tyrrhennian coast, archaeological excavations have never been able to confirm this information, and it has been proposed that a city from the time of the kings may have existed a bit farther up the Tiber. Investigations deep below the city of Ostia, however, clearly show that the city originated in the 4th century BC, after the conquest of Veii by Rome and its subsequent consolidation of control over the entire coast.

Ostia has always played a very important role in defense, and probably one of its first and most important duties was military control of the salt marshes that since ancient times had been located at the mouth of the Tiber (the name itself connects it to the river: *ostium* means mouth or outlet), where the waters became marshy and evaporated, leaving salt deposits. In ancient times, salt was a precious resource, both for conserving food and for tanning hides. Control of the salt marshes also meant control of the roads leading into this area, and the first settlement rose right at the intersection of these paths. It was a

castrum, with a town structure that closely followed that of a Roman military camp, with two main perpendicular roads, the *Decumanus* and the *Cardus Maximus*. It remained a *castrum* until the 3rd-2nd century BC, by which time it had outgrown its exclusively military functions. It became not only a naval base defending the capital, but also a port suburb, and changed its economic and political structure. Enclosures then became walls, the gates became architecture and the Forum was built at the intersection of the Cardus and Decumanus, a main square that became a meeting place for the diverse population that sources identify as the first Roman colony. While at first there were only

300 colonists, as time passed, the population of the town climbed as high as 50,000. Between the end of the 2nd and the beginning of the first century BC, new city walls were built that included a territory 30 times larger than that of the primitive *castrum* (although, according to normal town planning schemes, a great deal of green space was left between the actual town and the walls). Beginning in the early imperial age, a number of different facilities were gradually built in the city: the theater; the Piazzale delle Corporazioni, or the Guild Square; the aqueduct and the thermal baths. One of the greatest problems that had to be faced was bringing the port up to standard. The